AR-15 Carbine/Rifle Owner's Manual

By Erik Lawrence

ATTENTION US MILITARY UNITS, US GOVERNMENT AGENCIES AND PROFESSIONAL ORGANIZATIONS: Quantity discounts are available on bulk purchases of this book. Special books or book excerpts can also be created to fit specific needs. For information, please contact:

Vigilant Security Services®   Las Vegas, NV
vig-sec.com   support@vig-sec.com

Although the author and publisher have made every effort to ensure the accuracy and completeness of information contained in this book, we assume no responsibility for the use or misuse of information contained in this book, errors, inaccuracies, omissions, or any inconsistency herein. Portions of this manual are excerpts from outside sources but have been validated and modified as necessary.

First printing 2010

ISBN-13: 978-1-941998-72-4
LCCN: Not Yet Assigned

Firearms are potentially dangerous and must be handled responsibly by individuals. The technical information presented in this publication on the use of the weapon system reflects the author's research, beliefs, and experiences. The information in this book is presented for academic study only. Neither the author nor the publisher assumes any responsibility for the use or misuse of information contained in this book.

SAFETY NOTICE - Before starting an inspection, ensure the weapon is cleared. Do not manipulate the trigger until the weapon has been cleared of all ammunition. Inspect the chamber to ensure that it is empty, and no ammunition is present. Keep the weapon oriented in a safe direction when loading and handling.

AMMUNITION NOTICE- This weapon fires 5.56x45mm NATO (.223 Remington) ammunition. Firing the incorrect ammunition will damage the weapon and possibly injure the operator.

PROPER TRAINING - Training should be received from knowledgeable and experienced operators on this particular weapon system. Vigilant Security Services® Training provides this training and continually perfects its instruction with up-to-date information from actual use.

WARNING: IT IS YOUR RESPONSIBILITY TO ASSURE THAT YOUR FIREARM IS HANDLED, FIRED, AND STORED SAFELY AND RESPONSIBLY AT ALL TIMES.

This manual provides instructions on the operation and maintenance of your AR-15 firearm. Read and understand it carefully before you try to use your firearm. Your safety, and that of those around you, depends on your knowledge of your firearm and on your knowledge of safety rules common to all firearms. Please study the common-sense safety rules noted in this manual.

Your first responsibility as a gun owner is always safety!

Your second responsibility as a gun owner is security. Make sure that your firearm remains in responsible hands at all times! Don't become an unwitting partner in a crime or tragedy: make sure your firearm is properly secured. Lock it in a secure storage container or, if none is available, remove the bolt and bolt carrier assembly and store it separately. If you have more than one similar firearm, make sure that you specifically identify the removed assembly with its original firearm because the assemblies may not be interchangeable.

It is also your responsibility to assure that you comply with all federal, state, and local laws with regard to the purchase, ownership, use, and storage of your firearm.

NOTICE

Vigilant Security Services® has no control over the use of your firearm, and shall not be responsible for injury, death, or damage to property resulting from either intentional or accidental discharge of this firearm. In addition, Vigilant Security Services ® shall not be responsible for proper function of the firearm when it is used for purposes or subjected to treatment for which it was not intended. Vigilant Security Services ® will not honor claims which may result from careless or improper handling, unauthorized adjustments or parts replacement, corrosion, neglect, use of the wrong type or caliber of ammunition, or the use of ammunition other than original, high quality commercially manufactured ammunition in good condition or any combination thereof.

SAFETY FIRST! IT'S YOUR RESPONSIBILITY!

- ❖ Treat every gun as if it is loaded ...AT ALL TIMES!
- ❖ Always keep the muzzle pointed in a safe direction.
- ❖ Never point your firearm at anything that you do not intend to destroy.
- ❖ Keep your finger off the trigger and out of the trigger guard until you are aiming at your target and ready to shoot.
- ❖ Always keep the safety in the "SAFE" position, especially when the firearm is loaded and cocked, until you are ready to fire.
- ❖ Always keep and carry your firearm with an empty chamber until you intend to shoot, so that your firearm cannot be fired unintentionally. Firearms should be unloaded when not actually in use.
- ❖ Be sure of your target and backstop before you shoot. Ask yourself what your bullet will hit if it misses or goes through the target.
- ❖ Never shoot at hard, flat surfaces or water...bullets can ricochet.
- ❖ Always wear hearing and eye protection when shooting.
- ❖ Discharging firearms in poorly ventilated areas, cleaning firearms, or handling ammunition may result in exposure to lead, a substance known to be associated with birth defects, reproductive harm, and other serious injury. Have adequate ventilation at all times and wash hands after handling.
- ❖ Be sure that your barrel is clear of obstructions, including excessive oil, grease, cleaning patches, etc before shooting.
- ❖ Use only clean, high-quality factory loaded ammunition in good condition. Vigilant Security Services® does not condone the use of handloaded ammunition. Any such use voids the Vigilant Security Services® warranty.
- ❖ Do not alter or modify your firearm.
- ❖ Do not try to change your firearm's trigger pull, because alterations of trigger pull can affect sear engagement and might cause accidental firing.
- ❖ Store firearms and ammunition separately, and beyond children's reach.

IN CASE OF MALFUNCTION, STOP! REVIEW THIS MANUAL TO IDENTIFY AND RESOLVE THE PROBLEM. IF YOU CANNOT RESOLVE IT, CONTACT VIGILANT SECURITY SERVICES®.

KEEP THIS MANUAL WITH YOUR RIFLE. IF YOU SELL THE RIFLE, GIVE THIS MANUAL TO THE NEW OWNER.

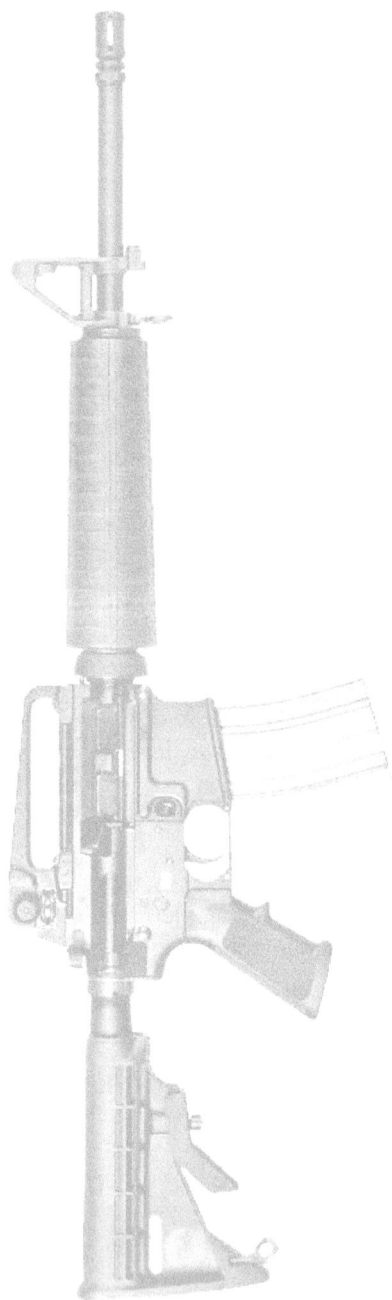

Table of Contents

General Information

Specifications

The AR-15 Carbine/Rifle is a .223 Remington/5.56x45mm lightweight air-cooled, gas-operated, magazine-fed, shoulder-fired rifle. The AR-15 fires from a closed bolt in semi-automatic mode while the military M4 variants are either semi-automatic, burst, or full-automatic.

AR-15A2 HBAR type rifle

CALIBER- .223 Remington or 5.56x45mm NATO
WEIGHT WITHOUT MAGAZINE- 8.5 pounds (2.94 kg)
EMPTY 30-ROUND MAGAZINE- 0.25 pounds (0.11 kg)
LOADED 30-ROUND MAGAZINE- 1 pound (0.45 kg)
OVERALL LENGTH- 39 inches (1 meter)
BARREL LENGTH- 20 inches (51 cm)
BORE CHARACTERISTICS- Hard chrome-lined, 6 Lands, 1:9
METHOD OF OPERATION- Gas-direct system; rotating bolt
MUZZLE VELOCITY- 3,200 feet/second (975 meters/second)
EFFECTIVE RANGE- 600 meters
FRONT SIGHT- Adjustable front
REAR SIGHT- M16A4 target-style sight adjustable for windage and elevation to 600 meters
SIGHT RADIUS- 20 inches (51 cm)
FIRE CONTROL SELECTION- Safe – Semi-automatic
UPPER RECEIVER- Flat top with detachable carrying handle

AR-15A2/A3 type carbine

CALIBER- .223 Remington or 5.56x45mm NATO
WEIGHT WITHOUT MAGAZINE- 7.0 pounds (3.2 kg)
EMPTY 30-ROUND MAGAZINE- 0.25 pounds (0.11 kg)
LOADED 30-ROUND MAGAZINE- 1 pound (0.45 kg)
LENGTH- 29.8 inches to 33 inches (collapsed/extended)
BARREL LENGTH- 16.1 inches (41 cm)
BORE CHARACTERISTICS- Hard chrome-lined, 6 Lands
METHOD OF OPERATION- Gas-direct system; rotating bolt
MUZZLE VELOCITY- 2800 feet/second (884 meters/second)
EFFECTIVE RANGE- 600 meters
FRONT SIGHT- Adjustable front
REAR SIGHT- Dual apertures (0-200m and 300-600) target-style sight adjustable for windage and elevation to 600 meters
SIGHT RADIUS- 14.5 inches (37 cm)
FIRE CONTROL SELECTION- Safe – Semi-automatic
UPPER RECEIVER-
> **A2 Model-** Non-removable carrying handle
> **A3 Model-** Flat top with detachable carrying handle

The barrel rifling twists vary from the original 1 turn in 12 inches (1/12) on the first AR-15 series guns shooting 55-grain bullets, to the current 1/7 or 1/9 twist on the M16A2/A4 service rifle and M4 Carbine. The faster twist is necessary to stabilize the longer and heavier SS109 62-grain bullet with steel penetrator used in M855 ammunition.

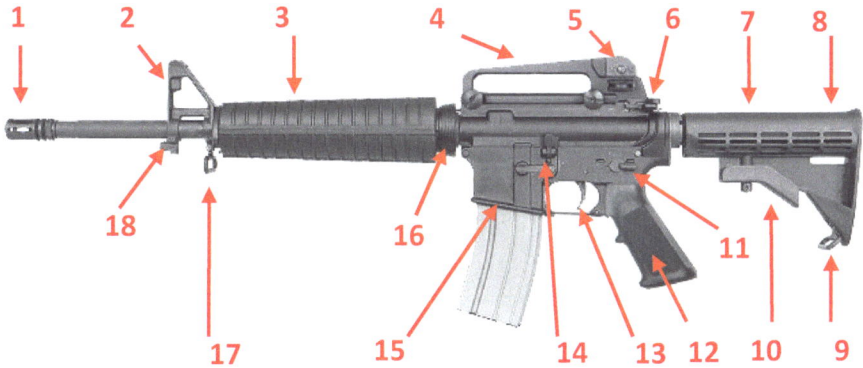

AR-15 Carbine Nomenclature – Left Side

1 – Muzzle/Flash Suppressor
2 – Front Sight Tower
3 – Handguard
4 – Carrying Handle
5 – Rear Sight
6 – Charging Handle
7 – Buffer Extension Tube (under stock)
8 – Buttstock
9 – Rear Sling Attachment

10 – Stock Adjustment Lever
11 – Safety
12 – Pistol Grip
13 – Trigger
14 – Bolt Release
15 – Magazine Well
16 – Slip Ring
17 – Front Sling Attachment
18 – Bayonet Lug

AR-15 Carbine Nomenclature – Right Side

19 – Magazine Release

Clearing the AR-15

Figure 1 – Safety/selector lever (on SAFE)

A. Ensure the rifle is on SAFE, refer to Figure 1. At all time during the clearing, you must never touch the trigger and keep the muzzle pointed in a safe direction. If the safety selector will not rotate to SAFE the hammer may be in the uncocked position, pull the charging handle to the rear and release. Reattempt to place rifle of SAFE.

Figure 2 – Unlocking the magazine and removing the magazine

B. Remove the magazine by pressing the magazine catch in on the right side of the receiver/magazine well and pull the magazine downward from the weapon to release it, refer to Figure 2. Place the magazine down or in a pouch.

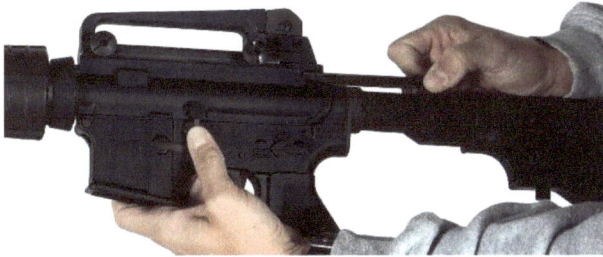

Figure 3 – Locking the bolt carrier to the rear

C. Extract the cartridge (if any) from the chamber. To lock the bolt open, pull the charging handle rearward, press the bottom of the bolt catch, and allow the bolt to move forward until the bolt catch stops it. Return the charging handle forward. Observe the round extracting and ejecting from the ejection port; do not attempt to retain the round, refer to Figure 3.

Figure 4 – Inspection of the chamber

D. Visually observe that there is no magazine in the rifle and no round in the chamber; physically check with your finger in low-light conditions as needed, refer to Figure 4.

NOTE- you must not reverse the steps listed above. If you clear and inspect the chamber prior to removing the magazine you will load another round into the chamber when you release the charging handle. Always check the safety position and remove the magazine prior to clearing the chamber.

Disassembling the AR-15

To ensure the proper function of the AR-15 it is necessary to disassemble the weapon to inspect and clean the internal components. The names of the parts should be learned through practice in disassembling and reassembling to enhance operator competence. Generally, the parts are named for the functions they perform, i.e., the trigger guard guards the trigger, the charging handle is used to charge the weapon, etc. We have broken down the disassembly into normal operator field strip and detailed armor disassembly. Stay within your ability level or have a friend who can put your rifle back together.

Figure 5 – AR-15

AR-15 rifle completely disassembled and ready for cleaning and inspection.

Figure 6 – Major Components of M16/AR-15/M4 rifles

Major Components of M16/AR-15/M4 rifles, refer to Figure 6

1 - Lower Receiver and Buttstock Assembly
2 - Upper Receiver and Barrel Assembly
3 - Charging Handle
4 - Bolt and Bolt Carrier Assembly

When the operator begins to disassemble the weapon, it should be done in the following order:

To begin the disassembly-

Upper and lower receivers

1. First clear the weapon as per the above description, depending on the weapon's condition.

2. Place the weapon on a flat, clean surface with the muzzle oriented in a safe direction. You may remove the sling if you need but otherwise you can leave it on the weapon.

Figure 7 – Separating the upper and lower receivers by pressing the take down pin

3. Separate the upper and lower receivers by grasping the weapon by the buttstock and with your free hand, push the take down pin as far as it will go right, do not force it, and then pull the pin from the right side until it stops, refer to Figure 7.

Figure 8 – Removing the pivot pin

4. Push the pivot pin as far as it will go right, do not force it, and then pull the pin from the right side until it stops, refer to Figure 8. Lay the separated receivers down.

Charging handle and bolt carrier assembly

Figure 9a – Removing the bolt assembly

5. Unlock and pull back the charging handle and bolt carrier assembly, refer to Figure 9a.

Figure 9b – Lift out the bolt assembly

6. Lift the bolt carrier assembly off the charging handle, refer to Figure 9b.

Figure 9c – Lift out the charging handle

7. Pull back and lift the charging handle, ensure you position the charging handle to clear the upper receiver's track, refer to Figure 9c.

Figure 10a – Components of the bolt carrier assembly

1. Firing Pin Retaining Pin
2. Firing Pin
3. Bolt Cam Pin

4. Bolt Assembly
5. Bolt Carrier

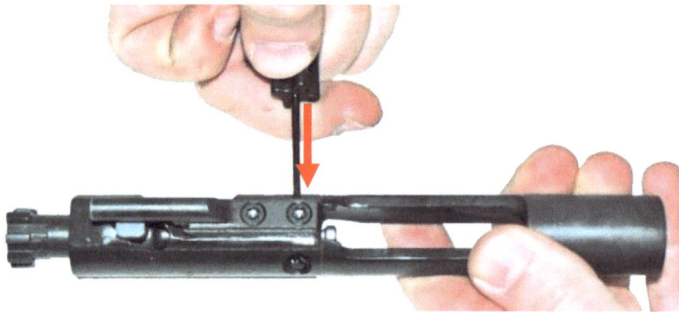

Figure 10b – Removing the firing pin retaining pin

8. Move the bolt forward to the unlocked position and remove the firing pin retaining pin, the Glock punch tool works great. Do not open or close the split end of the firing pin retaining pin, refer to Figure 10b.

Figure 10c – Locking the bolt to the rear

9. Push in on the bolt to put it in the rearward locked position, refer to Figure 10c.

Figure 10d – Removing the firing pin

10. Catch the firing pin as it drops out of the rear of the bolt carrier assembly, refer to Figure 10d.

Figure 10e – Removing the cam pin

11. Give the bolt cam pin a ¼ turn and lift it out, refer to Figure 10e.

Figure 10f – Removing the bolt from the bolt carrier.

12. Remove the bolt by pulling it from the front of the bolt carrier, refer to Figure 10f.

Figure 10g – Components of the bolt assembly

Components of the bolt

1- Extractor Pin	5- Ejector
2- Extractor	6- Ejector Spring
3- Extractor Spring	7- Gas Rings (3)
4- Ejector Pin	8- Bolt

Figure 10h – Checking extractor spring tension

13. Check the spring tension on the extractor by pressing on rear of it, refer to Figure 10h. Extractor claw should return once released. If you are to disassemble the extractor do is in the following manner.

Figure 10i – Removing the extractor pin

14. With a punch, Glock tool, cartridge head, or appropriate tool remove the extractor pin, refer to Figure 10i.

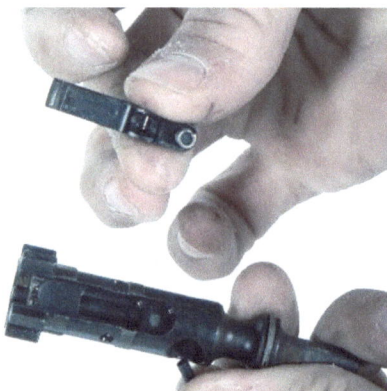

Figure 10j – Removing the extractor

15. Remove the extractor and spring assembly, refer to Figure 10j. Do not remove the spring assembly, its insert or the O-ring from the extractor unless you are upgrading this to a black buffer, five coil spring and O Ring to enhance the extraction capability.

Lower Receiver

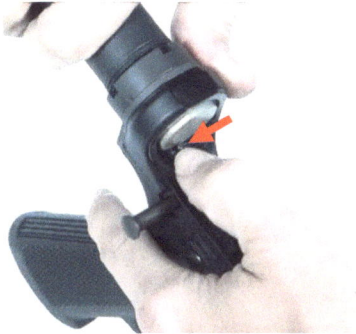

Figure 11a – Depressing the buffer spring retainer

16. The hammer must be in the cocked position. Cock the hammer with your thumb if needed. Push in the buffer and depress the retainer to release the buffer, refer to Figure 11a.

Figure 11b – Removing the buffer

17. Remove the buffer. The buffer is under tension so retain positive control of the buffer as you are removing it from the buffer tube, refer to Figure 11b.

18. Remove the handguards. The handguards can be removed by depressing the delta ring and lifting out the separate halves of the handguard.

19. This is the end of the operator disassembly of the weapon. **Prior to any further disassembly you should seek a qualified gunsmith to instruct you in this. We list the further disassembly for information purposes only.**

Cleaning and Lubrication

The AR-15 is a dependable rifle, but routine cleaning is advised to insure functionality. Clean the weapon as often as the situation dictates and the environment necessitates. Clean your rifle, keep it serviceable and know how it operates to make effect use of your time.

Keep the weapon free of dirt and dust as much as possible; use a muzzle cap or tape to keep them from the bore. Depending on the operating environment, keep lubricant only on metal-to-metal moving parts and use paintbrushes to clean dust and dirt off of and out of the weapon.

In hot and humid climates, inspect the weapon often for signs of rust. Keep the weapon free of moisture and keep a fine coat of lubricating oil on the metal surfaces. If the weapon is exposed to salt air, high humidity, or water, then clean and oil the weapon entirely as often as needed to keep it serviceable.

In hot and dry climates such as deserts, keep the weapon lubricated only on metal-to-metal moving parts and use paint brushes to clean dust and dirt off of and out of the weapon. Keeping the weapon free of unneeded oil will prevent sand and dust from collecting in the receiver and bore.

Keep your ammunition in containers when not in use and clean off the cartridges as necessary.

Clean the barrel with the cleaning rod or bore snake. Use solvent-lubricated brass brushes to break up carbon in the bore, and then use a solvent-covered patch to push the carbon out and a then dry patch until it is clean. The bores are chrome lined, so they clean up easily. A bore snake is a great bore-cleaning product to do this, as the barrel is clean with one pass of the bore snake.

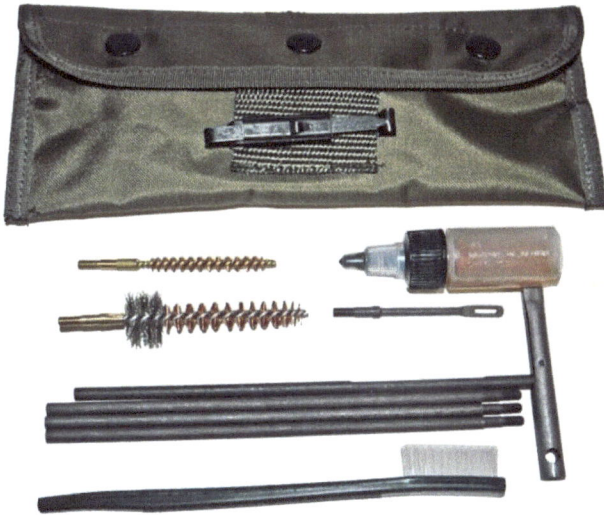

Figure 12 – Photo of cleaning items from standard cleaning kit

1- Metal rod sections – for pushing brushes or patches down the bore
2- Chamber brush – for cleaning the lug recess and chamber
3- Brass-bristled bore brush – to attach to the cleaning rod sections
4- Steel patch jag – to attach to the end of the cleaning rod sections
5- Rubber storage bag - used to store the cleaning kit in a M16A2 buttstock
6- All Purpose Brush – general cleaning and scrubbing
7- Patches, Cotton – removes carbon and oil from bore
8- Cleaning, Lubricant, and Protectant (CLP) – bottle of CLP

Upper Receiver Cleaning

Barrel cleaning tips
- Clean the bore from the chamber to muzzle direction.
- Do not reverse the direction of the bore brush while it is still in the bore (prevents ruining your brush), push it completely out then pull back through.
- Use cleaning solvent on the bore and chamber, the gas tube, the upper receiver and barrel assembly, locking lugs and all areas of powder fouling, corrosion, dirt or dust.

1. Use a cleaning rod, bore brush and cleaning solvent to break up initial carbon build up in bore. Run the rod through the chamber and flash suppressor several times.

Figure 13 – Example using the rod section and chamber brush to clean the chamber

2. Assemble the rod and chamber brush for chamber cleaning and break up the carbon in the chamber and lug recesses. Apply cleaning solvent and insert it into the chamber and lug recesses. Clean by pushing and twisting the cleaning rod, refer to Figure 13.

Figure 14 – Cleaning the gas tube

3. Use the multi-purpose brush or bore brush to clean the outside surface of the protruding gas tube, refer to Figure 14. Do not use a serviceable bore brush to do this. Do not clean the inside of the gas tube.

Figure 15 – Rod the bore from chamber to bore

4. Once the bore and chamber has been brushed replace the bore brush with the patch jag and use the cotton patches to remove the fouling from the bore and chamber area, refer to Figure 15. Change patches till the bore and chamber are no longer fouled. As with the bore brush, do not change direction until the patch and jag are out of the muzzle.

5. You may have to let the solvent sit on heavily build up carbon deposits. Scraping may be required for built up carbon.

Bolt Carrier Assembly and Charging Handle Cleaning

1. Clean all parts and surfaces with a GI general-purpose brush/toothbrush, rag and or swab saturated in powder cleaning solvent.

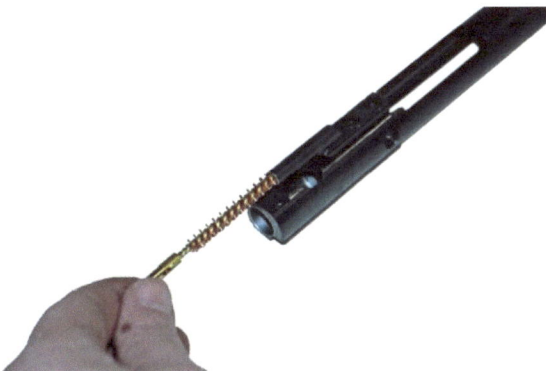

Figure 16 – Lightly clean the gas key with a worn bore brush

2. Clean the bolt carrier key with a worn bore brush dipped in solvent and dry with a pipe cleaner, refer to Figure 16

Figure 17 – Cleaning the bolt

3. Remove carbon deposits from the locking lugs with a general purpose or worn bore brush dipped in solvent, refer to Figure 17.

Figure 18 – Cleaning the carbon from the bolt

4. Clean the areas behind the bolt rings, refer to Figure 18

Figure 19 – Clean extractor groove and check sharpness

5. Clean under the lip if the extractor, remove all brass shavings, refer to Figure 19.

6. Press the ejector in repeatedly to remove accumulated brass shavings from the ejector hole and assure the ejector moves freely. Lubricate it generously. If the spring does not have a noticeable amount of spring tension - replace the extractor and spring.

7. Clean the carbon from the outside surfaces of the charging handle.

8. Clean the firing pin retaining pin and cam pin.

Lower Receiver Assembly

NOTE- Do not use wire type brushes or abrasive material to clean aluminum surfaces.

Figure 20 – Clean the lower receiver

1. Wipe and or brush dirt and sand from the trigger and trigger guard, refer to Figure 20.

2. Wipe and or brush powder fouling, corrosion and foreign matter from the lower receiver assembly.

3. Wipe with a solvent soaked rag the lower receiver, buffer and buffer spring.

4. Wipe with a dry rag or with pressurized air-dry the parts.

Lubrication

- **Do not use any lubricant containing graphite. Graphite can cause corrosion in aluminum alloys.**

- **Do not use any abrasive cleaners or wire brushes on the upper or lower receivers.**

Lubrication Tips:

1. Lightly lubricate the firing pin and firing pin recess in the bolt. (Figure 21)

Figure 21 – Bolt and firing pin lubrication points

2. Lubricate the outside of the bolt cam pin, and the firing pin retaining pin. Make certain to lubricate the bolt cam pin hole, bolt gas rings, and outside of the bolt, refer to Figure 21. Excess lube will be blown out with the first shot so there is no need to over lubricate.

Figure 22 – Bolt carrier lubrication points

3. Lightly lubricate the inner and outer surfaces of the bolt carrier. Generously lubricate the slide and cam pin area of the bolt carrier, refer to Figure 22.

4. Lightly lubricate the charging handle.

5. Dry the bolt carrier key tube with a pipe cleaner. Note: DO NOT excessively attempt to scrap the carbon deposits on the inside of the carrier as you can damage it.

6. Lightly lubricate the recoil spring and buffer.

7. Lubricate takedown pins and the inside parts (where metal moves on metal only) of the lower receiver.

8. Lightly lubricate the bore and chamber with a lightly lubricated patch on the cleaning rod.

9. Lubricate the locking lugs.

10. Apply a drop of lubricant onto the front sight detent and depress to ensure it works properly.

Firearm specific cleaners and lubricants are best to use. However, spray carburetor cleaner (in well ventilated areas) is very useful for removing carbon buildup in the upper receiver and bolt carrier assemblies. In areas where weapon specific cleaners and lubricants cannot be obtained, testing by Rock Island Arsenal has found that Automatic Transmission Fluid can be safely used as a cleaner and light lubricant. Also, 20-weight synthetic motor oil can be used as a lubricant with no harmful effects to the weapon.

Lube all operating parts. Inside the receiver, go ahead and coat the metal in a light film of CLP or light machine/gun oil. Some type of grease TW-25B can be used on the metal to metal (shiny spots) to allow the rifle to operate smoothly.

Protection

Use a type of Cleaner/Lubricant/Protectant (CLP). When not available some prefer motor oil, automatic transmission fluid, or light gun oil. With a rag, wipe down all exposed metal with CLP, interior and exterior, parkerized, blued, or otherwise. A slight film is all that is required to protect the gun.

Assembling the AR-15

As you are assembling the M4 rifle, reinspect the internal parts to ensure that each is in working order.

Lower Receiver Assembly

Figure 23 – Inserting the buffer and buffer spring

1. Insert the buffer and buffer spring into the buffer tube and push past the buffer retaining pin by depressing it, refer to Figure 23.

Bolt Carrier Assembly and Charging Handle

Figure 24 –line up the extractor to insert extractor pin

2. Extractor- If the extractor spring comes loose from the extractor; seat the large end of the extractor spring in the extractor. Ensure the reinforcement ring is around the spring. Insert the extractor with

spring assembly into bolt. Push extractor until the holes on the extractor and bolt are aligned and insert the extractor pin, refer to Figure 24.

3. Gas rings on bolt- staggering them does nothing to help prevent the loss of any gas, when inserted into the carrier they are compressed flush, refer to Figure 25.

Figure 25 – Gas ring compress once inserted into the bolt carrier - simulated

4. Slide the bolt assembly into the bolt carrier, far enough to insert the cam pin. Ensure you have the bolt with the extractor on the right side so the cam pin hole will line up for cam pin insertion.

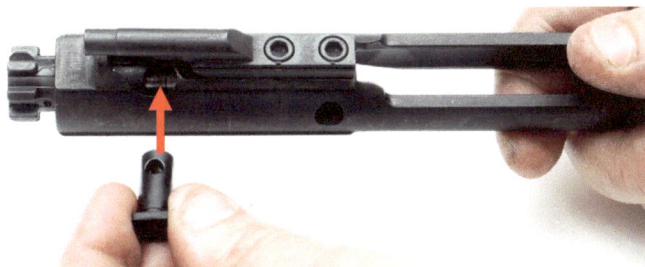

Figure 26 – Insert the cam pin into the bolt carrier (line up the bolt)

5. Insert the bolt cam pin and give it a ¼ turn, refer to Figure 26.

Figure 27 – Insert the firing pin into the rear of the bolt

6. Drop the firing pin into its opening, refer to Figure 27.

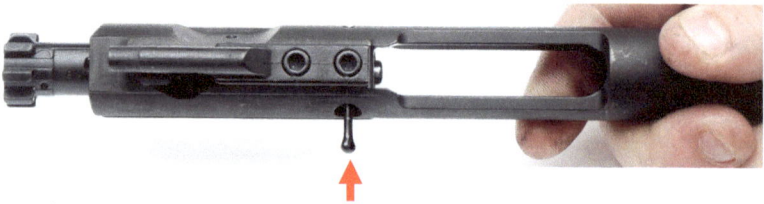

Figure 28 – Insert the firing pin retaining pin in the bolt carrier

7. Pull the bolt assembly forward and insert the firing pin retaining pin in the area between the large flange and the blunt end of the firing pin, refer to Figure 28.

Figure 29 – Checking for firing pin retention

8. Turn the bolt carrier assembly up and attempt to shake out the firing pin. The firing pin must not fall out. If the firing pin does fall out, remove the firing pin retaining pin, reinsert the firing pin fully and reinsert the firing pin retaining pin. Recheck for proper assembly, the weapon will not fire with the retaining pin not properly holding in the firing pin, refer to Figure 29.

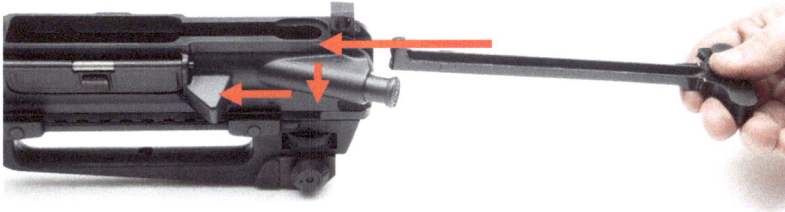

Figure 30 – Inserting the charging handle into the upper receiver

9. Place the charging handle into the upper receiver and engage the handle's lugs with the track in the receiver, then push the charging handle part way into the upper receiver, refer to Figure 30.

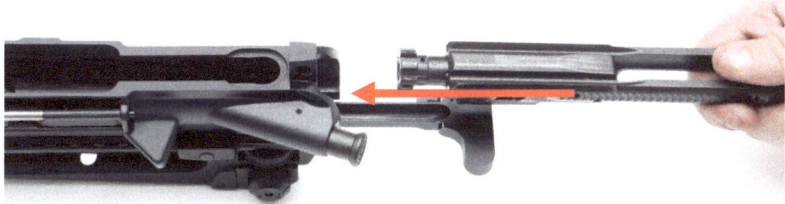

Figure 31 – Inserting the bolt carrier assembly into the upper receiver

10. Slide the bolt carrier assembly, bolt extended, into the upper receiver, refer to Figure 31.

Figure 32 – Locking the assembly into the receiver

11. Push the charging handle assembly and bolt carrier assembly together into the upper receiver, refer to Figure 32.

Figure 33 – Pushing in the pivot pin

12. Align the upper and lower receivers. Align the pivot pin holes with the pivot pin and push the front pivot pin in. Note the hammer must be in the cocked position; press it down with your thumb to cock, refer to Figure 33.

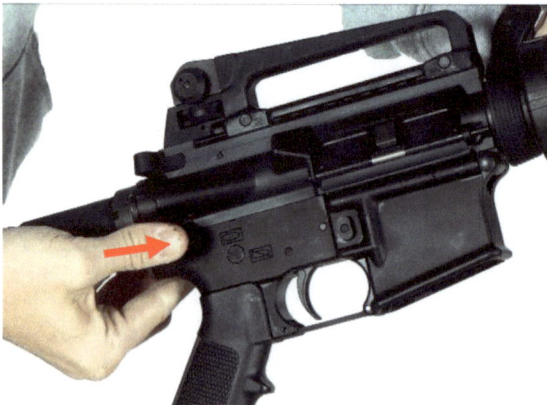

Figure 34 – Pushing in the takedown pin

13. Close the upper and lower receivers. Push in the rear takedown pin, refer to Figure 34.

Figure 35 – Removing the handguards

14. If you have removed your handguards use a buddy system or grow a third arm to fight them back on, refer to Figure 35.
    a. Place the weapon on its buttstock with one hand gripping the stock. Insert one handguard into the hand guard cap at the top.
    b. Press down or use a handguard tool to press down on the slip ring and install one rear of the handguard under the slip ring.
    c. Repeat these steps to install the second handguard.

Figure 36 – Attaching the sling

15. Reattach your sling if you removed it prior to disassembly, refer to Figure 36.

Function Check Procedures

Safety and function Check:

1. Ensure the weapon is clear of all ammunition and pointed in a safe direction.

2. Pull charging handle to rear and release it. Place selector on SAFE. Squeeze the trigger and the hammer should not fall.

3. Place the selector on FIRE. Squeeze the trigger and hold the trigger to the rear. The hammer should fall. While holding the trigger to the rear pull the charging handle to the rear and release it. Release the trigger and you should hear a click as you release the trigger. Squeeze the trigger again; the hammer should fall.

4. Pull charging handle to rear again, release then place the weapon on SAFE.

NOTE- If your rifle fails any of these tests then check your assembly. If the rifle will not pass these checks and it has been assembled properly, contact Vigilant Security Services® or a qualified gunsmith for assistance.

How to Disassemble an M16/M4 Magazine

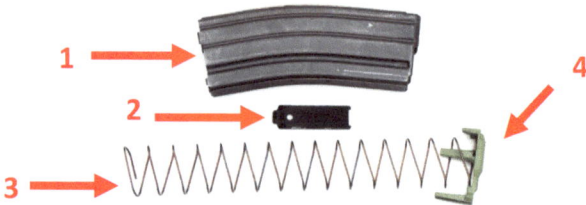

Figure 37 Parts of a typical 30 round M4 magazine

1- Magazine body	3- Spring
2- Magazine floor plate	4- Follower

To disassemble the magazine, ensure the magazine is unloaded, with no ammo.

Figure 38a and 38b – Magazine floorplate removal

1- Use a bullet or pointed object to depress the retaining plate through the floor plate and start to slide the floor plate to the rear. The older, dirtier, and/or rusty the magazine is, the harder this step will be to do. Be careful not to slide the floor plate fully off until you are ready to apply pressure to the retainer plate, as it is under spring tension, refer to Figure 38a.

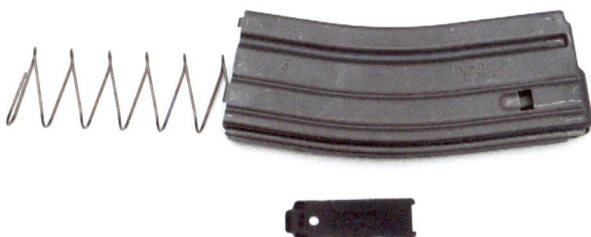

Figure 39a – Magazine partial disassembled

Figure 39b – Magazine completely disassembled

2- Once you have the floor plate started, use your thumb to hold the retainer plate and remove the floor plate fully. Now you can release the spring tension in a controlled manner and remove the spring and follower from the magazine body. The follower and retaining plate can be removed from the spring if needed for thorough cleaning, refer to Figure 39.

It is very important to clean the inside of the magazine body and the outside of the follower. Keep the magazine as dry as possible but lightly coated with a protectant to prevent rusting.

To reassemble, just reverse the process.

Loading the 20 or 30-round magazine

Ensure the magazines are clean, rust free, and without damage. Observe basic safety precautions of handling small arms ammunition at all times.

Ensure you have 5.56 x 45mm ammunition; this ammunition is easily confused for with 5.45 x 39mm (AK74). Inspect it for uniformity, cleanliness, and serviceability. Check all for undented primers and only use issued ammunition.

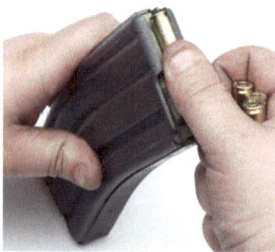  

Figure 40a   Figure 40b   Figure 40c
Magazine hand loading procedure

A. Use your non-dominant hand to hold the magazine with the front of the magazine toward your fingertips, refer to Figure 40a. With your dominant hand, one at a time, place the cartridge over the top of the magazine follower between the feed lips and press the cartridge straight down until it snaps under the feed lips, refer to Figure 40b. Once the cartridge is under the lip of the magazine body, slide it fully to the rear so the next round will be able to be pushed down, refer to Figure 40c.

B. The magazine can hold 30 cartridges, but due to the possibility of having to load with the bolt carrier forward we prefer to load 29 and then load the chamber so you have 28 in the magazine and one in the chamber and 28-round magazines loaded in your pouches, just personal preference. It is easiest to lay out the number of rounds for each magazine, so you don't have to count the rounds as you load the magazine or just strip two off a stripper clip in the set of three.

Loading the AR-15

NOTE: Keep the weapon oriented in a safe direction.

Clear the weapon as described in the previous section.

Loading from the open bolt

Figure 41 – Preparing to load the rifle

1. Lock the bolt carrier to the rear by pulling the charging handle fully to the rear, press and hold the bottom of the bolt lock lever, release tension on the charging handle and return it forward to its locked position. Place the safety, located on the left-hand side of the weapon, to the (SAFE) position. NOTE-The weapon will not go onto safe if the hammer is not cocked, refer to Figure 41.

Figure 42a	Figure 42b

Inserting the magazine into the rifle's magazine well and checking lock up

2. Insert the top of the magazine into the magazine well (bullets towards end of muzzle) and press the magazine upwards to lock it in, refer to Figure 42a. Ensure it is locked into place by slightly tugging down on it, refer to Figure 42b.

Do not abuse your magazines by loading 30 rounds and slamming it into a rifle with the bolt forward.

Figure 43 – Chambering a round – press the bolt release

3. Depress the upper portion of the bolt catch to release the bolt, refer to Figure 43. Tap the forward assist and close the dust cover. A checking of the magazine to ensure chambering can be done by removing the magazine and looking to see if the round on top is on the opposite side from when first inserted prior to chambering and or unlock and observe by slightly retracting the charging handle until you see or feel the brass of the cartridge, release the charging handle and once again tapping the forward assist to ensure the bolt is in battery.

Loading from the closed bolt

Figure 44a – Insert magazine

Figure 44b – Ensure it is locked in

1. Insert magazine until magazine catch engages, refer to Figure 44a. Pull down slightly to assure proper lock up, refer to Figure 44b. NEVER force or pound the magazine into the receiver. Fully loaded magazine may not want to lock into the magazine catch; one round should be removed to allow for easier lock up.

Figure 44c – Charging the rifle

2. Pull the charging handle fully back and release with your non-dominant hand. As the bolt travels forward by the weapons spring tension, it will strip the top round from the magazine and force it into the chamber, refer to Figures 44a, 44b and 44c. It is a good habit of tapping the forward assist to ensure the bolt is fully forward and in battery. Riding the charging handle forward will not allow for the bolt to fully return to battery.

Figure 45 – Safety/Selector on SAFE

3. If you are preparing the rifle to fire, it is now ready; otherwise, ensure the selector is in the safe position, refer to Figure 45. **Keep the safety on SAFE until you have the intention to shoot.**

Figure 46a – Press check

Press Check procedure-
To check if the chamber was loaded with a round, with the safety still engaged, pull the charging handle back slightly to see the casing being pulled from the chamber, refer to Figure 46. Once you have seen or felt the casing in the chamber return the charging handle forward and tap the forward assist to ensure the bolt is in battery. In low-light, you may have to reach in and feel the cartridge casing to ensure the chamber is loaded.

Figure 46b – Forward assist usage

Firing the AR-15

Orient toward the desired area/target, take a proper sight alignment and sight picture, rotate the selector/safety lever 90° to the FIRE position and press the trigger straight to the rear without interrupting your sight alignment and sight picture.

Once your target engagement is complete, rotate the selector to the rear safe position (up).

Basic Rifle Fundamentals

The shooter must understand and apply the four key fundamentals before he approaches the firing line. He must establish a steady position allowing observation of the target. He must aim the rifle at the target by aligning the sight system and fire the rifle without disturbing this alignment by improper breathing or during trigger squeeze. These skills are known collectively as the four fundamentals. Applying these four fundamentals rapidly and consistently is the integrated act of firing.

a. **Steady Position.** When the shooter approaches the firing line, he should assume a comfortable, steady firing position. The time and supervision each shooter has on the firing line is limited. He must learn how to establish a steady position during integrated act of dry-fire training. Dry firing is the practice of "firing" a firearm without ammunition. That is, to pull the trigger and allow the hammer or striker to drop on an empty chamber. The firer is the best judge of the quality of his position. If he can hold the front sight post steady through the fall of the hammer, he has a good position.

The steady position elements are as follows, refer to Figure 47.
(1) *Nonfiring Handgrip.* The rifle hand guard rests on the heel of the hand in the V formed by the thumb and fingers. The grip of the non-firing hand is light.

(2) *Rifle Butt Position.* The butt of the rifle is placed in the pocket of the firing shoulder. This reduces the effect of recoil and helps ensure a steady position.

(3) *Firing Handgrip.* The firing hand grasps the pistol grip, so it fits the V formed by the thumb and forefinger. The forefinger is placed on the trigger so the lay of the rifle is not disturbed when the trigger is squeezed. A slight rearward pressure is exerted by the remaining three fingers to ensure that the butt of the stock remains in the pocket of the shoulder, minimizing the effect of recoil.

(4) *Firing Elbow Placement.* The firing elbow is important in providing balance. Its exact location depends on the firing/fighting position used. Placement should allow shoulders to remain level.

(5) *Nonfiring Elbow.* The non-firing elbow is positioned firmly under the rifle to allow a comfortable and stable position. When the shooter engages a wide sector of fire, moving targets, and targets at various elevations, his non-firing elbow should remain free from support.

(6) *Cheek-to-Stock Weld.* The stock weld should provide a natural line of sight through the center of the rear sight aperture to the front sight post and on to the target. The firer's neck should be relaxed, allowing his cheek to fall naturally onto the stock. Through dry-fire training, the shooter practices this position until he assumes the same cheek-to-stock weld each time he assumes a given position, which provides consistency in aiming. Proper eye relief is obtained when a shooter establishes a good cheek-to-stock weld. A small change in eye relief normally occurs each time that the firer assumes a different firing position. The shooter should begin by trying to touch the charging handle with his nose when assuming a firing position. This will aid the shooter in maintaining the same cheek-to-stock weld hold each time the weapon is aimed. The shooter should be mindful of how the nose touches the charging handle and should be consistent when doing so. This should be critiqued and reinforced during dry-fire training.

Figure 47 – Steady position

(7) **Support.** When artificial support (sandbags, logs, stumps) is available, it should be used to steady the position and support the rifle. If it is not available, then the bones, not the muscles, in the firer's upper body must support the rifle.

(8) **Muscle Relaxation.** If support is used properly, the shooter should be able to relax most of his muscles. Using artificial support or bones in the upper body as support allows him to relax and settle into position. Using muscles to support the rifle can cause it to move due to muscle fatigue.

(9) **Natural Point of Aim.** When the shooter first assumes his firing position, he orients his rifle in the general direction of his target. Then he adjusts his body to bring the rifle and sights exactly in line with the desired aiming point. When using proper support and consistent cheek to stock weld the shooter should have his rifle and sights aligned naturally on the target. When correct body-rifle-target alignment is achieved, the front sight post must be held on target, using muscular support and effort. As the rifle fires, muscles tend to relax, causing the front sight to move away from the target toward the natural point of aim. Adjusting this point to the desired point of aim eliminates this movement. When multiple target exposures are expected (or a sector of fire must be covered), the shooter adjusts his natural point of aim to the center of the expected target exposure area (or center of sector).

b. **Aiming.** Having mastered the task of holding the rifle steady, the shooter must align the rifle with the target in exactly the same way for each firing. The firer is the final judge as to where his eye is focused. The instructor or trainer emphasizes this point by having the firer focus on the target and then focus back on the front sight post. He checks the position of the firing eye to ensure it is in line with the rear sight aperture.

(1) **Rifle Sight Alignment.** Alignment of the rifle with the target is critical. It involves placing the tip of the front sight post in the center of the rear sight aperture, refer to Figure 48. Any alignment error between the front and rear sights repeats itself for every 1/2 meter the bullet travels. For example, at the 25-meter line, any error in rifle alignment is multiplied 50 times. If the bullet is misaligned by 1/10 inch, it causes a target at 300 meters to be missed by 5 feet.

Figure 48 – Correct sight alignment

(2) ***Focus of the Eye.*** A proper firing position places the eye directly in line with the center of the rear sight aperture. When the eye is focused on the front sight post, the natural ability of the eye to center objects in a circle and to seek the point of greatest light (center of the aperture) aid in providing correct sight alignment. For the average shooter firing at combat-type targets, the natural ability of the eye can accurately align the sights. Therefore, the firer can place the tip of the front sight post on the aiming point, but the eye must be focused on the tip of the front sight post. This causes the target to appear blurry, while the front sight post is seen clearly. Two reasons for focusing on the front sight post are:

(a) Only a minor aiming error should occur since the error reflects only as much as the shooter fails to determine the target center. A greater aiming error can result if the front sight post is blurry due to focusing on the target or other objects.

(b) Focusing on the tip of the front sight post aids the firer in maintaining proper sight alignment, refer to Figure 49.

(3) ***Sight Picture.*** Once the shooter can correctly align his sights, he can obtain a sight picture. A correct sight picture has the target, front sight post, and rear sight aligned. The sight picture includes two basic elements: sight alignment and placement of the aiming point.

(a) Placement of the aiming point varies, depending on the engagement range. For example, refer to Figure 49 shows a silhouette at 300 meters where the aiming point is the center of mass, and the sights are aligned for a correct sight picture.

Figure 49 – Correct sight picture

(b) A technique to obtain a good sight picture is the side aiming technique, refer to Figure 50. It involves positioning the front sight post to the side of the target in line with the vertical center of mass, keeping the sights aligned. The front sight post is moved horizontally until the target is directly centered on the front sight post.

Figure 50 – Side aiming technique

(4) **Front Sight**. The front sight post is vital to proper firing and should be replaced when damaged. The post should be blackened anytime it

is shiny since precise focusing on the tip of the front sight post cannot be done otherwise.

(5) **Aiming Practice**. Aiming practice is conducted before firing live rounds. During day firing, the shooter should practice sight alignment and placement of the aiming point. Using training aids such as the M15A1 aiming card can do this.

c. **Breath Control.** As the firer's skills improve and as timed or multiple targets are presented, he must learn to control his breath at any part of the breathing cycle. Two types of breath control techniques are practiced during dry fire. The coach/trainer ensures that the firer uses two breathing techniques and understands them by instructing him to exaggerate his breathing. The firer must be aware of the rifle's movement (while sighted on a target) as a result of breathing.

(1) The first technique is used during zeroing (and when time is available to fire a shot), refer to Figure 51. There is a moment of natural respiratory pause while breathing when most of the air has been exhaled from the lungs and before inhaling. Breathing should stop after most of the air has been exhaled during the normal breathing cycle. The shot must be fired before the shooter feels any discomfort.

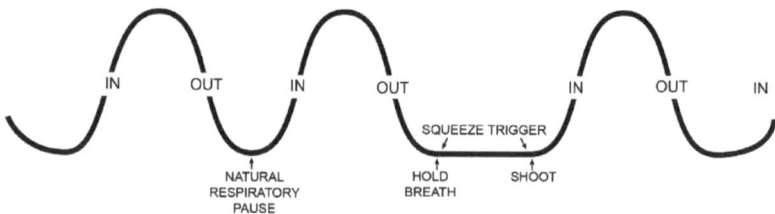

Figure 51 – Breath control for engaging single targets.

(2) The second breath control technique is employed during rapid fire (short-exposure targets), refer to Figure 52. Using this technique, the shooter stops his breath when he is about to squeeze the trigger.

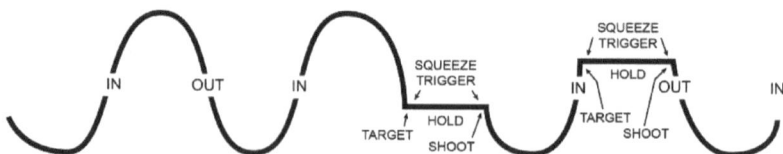

Figure 52 – Breath control while engagement of short-exposure targets

d. **Trigger Squeeze.** A novice firer can learn to place the rifle in a steady position and to correctly aim at the target if he follows the basic principles. If the trigger is not properly squeezed, the rifle will be misaligned with the target at the moment of firing.

(1) *Rifle Movement.* Trigger squeeze is important for two reasons: First, any sudden movement of the finger on the trigger can disturb the lay of the rifle and cause the shot to miss the target. Second, the precise instant of firing should be a surprise to the shooter. The shooter's natural reflex to compensate for the noise and slight punch in the shoulder can cause him to miss the target if he knows the exact instant the rifle will fire. The shooter usually tenses his shoulders when expecting the rifle to fire. It is difficult to detect since he does not realize he is flinching. When the hammer drops on a dummy round and does not fire, the shooter's natural reflexes demonstrate that he is improperly squeezing the trigger.

(2) *Trigger Finger.* The trigger finger (index finger on the firing hand) is placed on the trigger between the first joint and the tip of the finger (not the extreme end) and adjusted depending on hand size, grip, and so on. The trigger finger must squeeze the trigger to the rear so the hammer falls without disturbing the lay of the rifle. When a live round is fired, it is difficult to see what effect trigger pull had on the lay of the rifle. It is important to experiment with many finger positions during dry-fire training to ensure the hammer is falling with little disturbance to the aiming process.

(a) As the firer's skills increase with practice, he needs less time spent on trigger squeeze. Novice firers can take five seconds to perform an adequate trigger squeeze, but, as skills improve, he can squeeze the trigger in a second or less. The proper trigger squeeze should start with slight pressure on the trigger during the initial aiming process. The firer applies more pressure after the front sight post is steady on the target and he is holding his breath.

(b) The coach/trainer observes the trigger squeeze, emphasizes the correct procedure, and checks the firer's applied pressure. He places his finger on the trigger and has the firer squeeze the trigger by applying pressure to the coach/trainer's finger. The coach/trainer ensures that the firer squeezes straight to the rear on the trigger avoiding a left or right twisting movement. The coach/trainer observes that the firer follows through and holds the trigger to the rear for approximately one second after the round has been fired. A steady position reduces disturbance of the rifle during trigger squeeze.

(c) Wobble area is the movement of the front sight around the aiming point when the rifle is in the steadiest position. From an unsupported position, the firer experiences a greater wobble area than from a supported position. If the front sight strays from the target during the firing process, pressure on the trigger should be held constant and resumed as soon as sighting is corrected. The position must provide for the smallest possible wobble area. From a supported position, there should be minimal wobble area and little reason to detect movement. If movement of the rifle causes the front sight to leave the target, more practice is needed. The firer should never try to quickly squeeze the trigger while the sight is on the target. The best firing performance results when the trigger is squeezed continuously, and the rifle is fired without disturbing its lay.

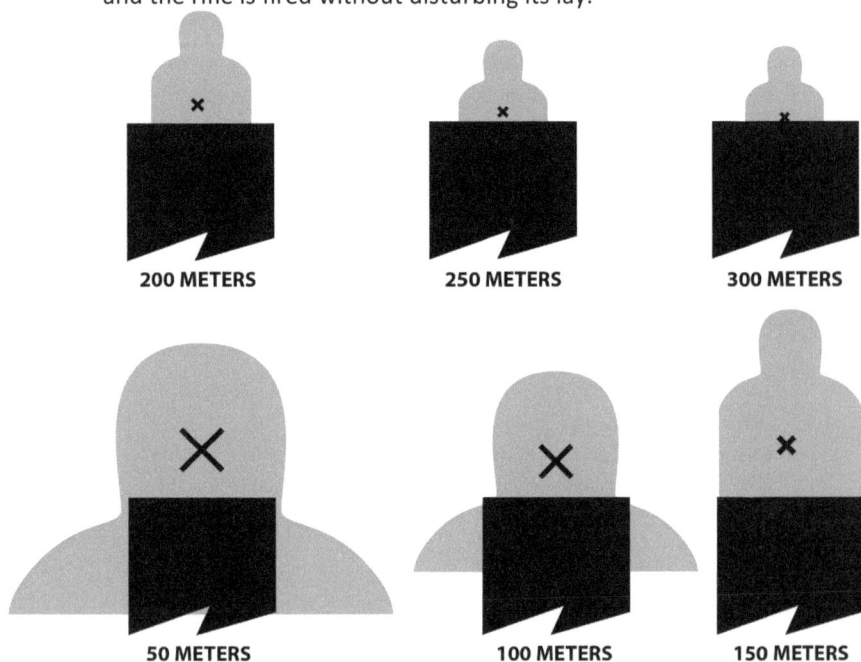

| 200 METERS | 250 METERS | 300 METERS |

| 50 METERS | 100 METERS | 150 METERS |

Figure 53 – AR-15 aiming point for a 25 meter zero

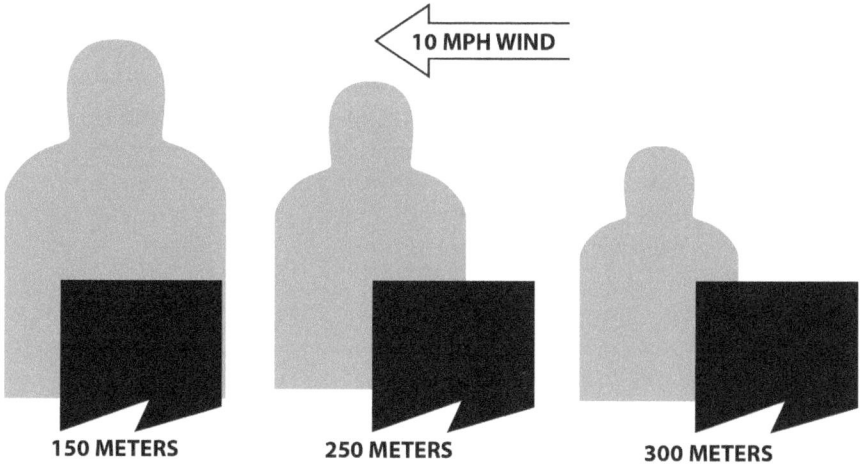

Figure 54 – AR-15 adjusted aiming point based on wind speed

Malfunctions / Troubleshooting

Malfunction and Immediate Action Procedures

A malfunction is a failure of the weapon to function properly. Defective ammunition or improper operation of the weapon by an operator is not considered a malfunction of the weapon. Malfunctions are caused by procedural or mechanical failures of the rifle, magazine, or ammunition. Pre-firing checks and serviceability inspections identify potential problems before they become malfunctions.

Sluggish operation and the corrective action: Sluggish operation (gun fires very slowly) of the weapon is usually due to excessive friction caused by dirt or carbon, lack of proper lubrication, burred parts or excessive loss of gas. To correct this problem you must disassemble, clean, and lubricate the weapon while inspecting the parts for burrs or damage. Replace parts as necessary.

Stoppages: A stoppage is an interruption in the cycle of operation caused by a faulty gun or ammunition. In short, the gun stops firing. A stoppage must be cleared quickly by applying immediate action.

Immediate Action - This is the prompt action taken by the gunner to reduce a stoppage of the rifle without investigating the cause. If the gun stops firing, the shooter performs immediate action. Hang fire and cook off are two terms that describe ammunition condition and should be understood in conjunction with immediate-action procedures.

Hang Fire: Occurs when the cartridge primer has detonated after being struck by the firing pin, but some problem with the propellant powder causes it to burn too slowly, and this delays the firing of the projectile. Time (5 seconds) is allotted for this malfunction before investigating a stoppage further because of potential injury to personnel and damage to equipment.

Cook Off: Occurs when the heat of the weapon is high enough to cause the propellant powder inside the round to ignite even though the primer has not been struck. Immediate action is to unload the weapon immediately and allow it cool prior to reloading and firing.

Malfunctions, Probable Causes, and Corrective Actions

1. Failure to Feed, Chamber, or Lock. A malfunction can occur when loading the rifle or during the cycle of operation. Once the magazine has been loaded into the rifle, the forward movement of the bolt carrier group could lack enough force (generated by the expansion of the action spring) to feed, chamber, or lock the bolt.

Probable Causes. The cause could be the result of one or more of the following:
- Excess accumulation of dirt or fouling in and around the bolt and bolt carrier.
- Defective magazine (dented, bulged, or a weak magazine spring).
- Improperly loaded magazine.
- Defective round (projectile forced back into the cartridge case, which could result in a stubbed round or the base of the previous cartridge could be separated, leaving the remainder in the chamber).
- Damaged or broken action spring.
- Exterior accumulation of dirt in the lower receiver extension.
- Fouled gas tube resulting in short recoil.
- A magazine resting on the ground or pushed forward could cause an improper lock.

Corrective Action. Applying immediate action usually corrects the malfunction. To avoid the risk of further jamming, the firer should watch for ejection of a cartridge and ensure that the upper receiver is free of any loose rounds. If immediate action fails to clear the malfunction, remedial action must be taken. The carrier should not be forced. If resistance is encountered, which can occur with an unserviceable round, the bolt should be locked to the rear, the magazine removed, and the malfunction cleared. For example, a bolt override is when a cartridge has wedged itself between the bolt and charging handle. The best way to correct this problem is by
- Ensuring the charging handle is pushed forward and locked in place.
- Securing the rifle and pulling the bolt to the rear until the bolt seats completely into the buffer well.
- Turning the rifle upright and allowing the overridden cartridge to fall out.

2. Failure to Fire Cartridge. This is a failure of a cartridge to fire despite the fact that a round has been chambered, the trigger pulled, and the sear released the hammer. This occurs when the firing pin fails to strike the primer with enough force or when the ammunition is defective.

Immediate action: This action is performed when the operator has a failure to fire, which is when the trigger is pulled, the hammer moves forward, and the weapon does not fire.

SPORTS- Type I, Failure to Fire
- **S**lap up on the bottom of the magazine

- **P**ull the charging handle to the rear

- **O**bserve the chamber for an ejection of the round

- **R**elease the charging handle

- **T**ap the forward assist

- **S**queeze the trigger again

If during your recharging of the action you observe a cartridge case or a round that is not ejected, then perform remedial action.

Remedial Action: When immediate action fails to reduce the stoppage, remedial action must be taken. To do so tactically is to release the magazine; recharge the action 3-4 times, watching for the round to be extracted and ejected; reload the magazine into the weapon; charge the rifle; and attempt to refire. Administratively prior to investigating the cause of the stoppage, you must clear the weapon, and this step may involve some disassembly of the weapon and replacement of parts to correct the problem. Remedial actions for stoppages are as follows.

Probable Causes. Excessive carbon buildup on the firing pin is often the cause, because the full forward travel of the firing pin is restricted. A defective or worn firing pin can give the same results. Inspection of the ammunition could reveal a shallow indentation or no mark on the primer, indicating a firing pin malfunction. Cartridges that show a normal indentation on the primer, but did not fire indicate faulty ammunition.

Corrective Action. If the malfunction continues, the firing pin, bolt, carrier, and locking lug recesses of the barrel extension should be inspected and any accumulation of excessive carbon or fouling should be removed. The firing pin should also be inspected for damage. Cartridges that show a normal indentation on the primer but failed to fire could indicate a bad ammunition lot. Those that show a complete penetration of the primer by the firing pin could also indicate failure of the cartridge to fully seat in the chamber.

NOTE: If the round is suspected to be faulty, it is reported and returned to the agency responsible for issuing ammunition.

WARNING If an audible "POP" or reduced recoil occurs during firing, immediately cease-fire. This POP or reduced recoil could be the result of a round being fired without enough force to send the projectile out of the barrel. Do not apply immediate action. Remove the magazine, lock the bolt to the rear, and place the selector lever in the safe position. Visually inspect the bore to ensure a projectile is not lodged in the barrel. If a projectile is lodged in the barrel, do not try to remove it. Turn the rifle in to the armorer.

1. **Failure to Extract.** A failure to extract results when the cartridge case remains in the chamber of the rifle. This creates a serious stoppage/malfunction when the bolt and bolt carrier recoils fully to the rear and upon if return forward strips a live round out of the magazine and forces it into the case already stuck in the chamber. This malfunction is one of the hardest to clear.

WARNING A failure to extract is considered an extremely serious malfunction, requiring the use of tools to clear. A live round could be left in the chamber and accidentally discharged. If a second live round is fed into the primer of the chambered live round, the rifle could explode and cause personal injury. This malfunction must be properly identified and reported. Failures to eject, definition on next page, should not be reported as extraction failures.

Probable Cause. Short recoil cycles and fouled or corroded rifle chambers are the most common causes of failures to extract. A damaged extractor or a weak or broken extractor spring can also cause this malfunction.

Corrective Action. The severity of a failure to extract determines the corrective action procedures. If the bolt has moved rearward far enough to strip a live round from the magazine in its forward motion, the bolt and carrier must be locked to the rear. The magazine and all loose rounds must be removed before clearing the stoppage. Usually, tapping the butt of the rifle on a hard surface causes the cartridge to fall out of the chamber. However, if the cartridge case is ruptured, it can be seized. When this occurs, a cleaning rod can be inserted into the bore from the muzzle end. The cartridge case can be forced from the chamber by tapping the cleaning rod against the inside base of the fired cartridge. If cleaning and inspecting the mechanism and chamber reveals no defects but failures to extract persist, the extractor and extractor spring should be replaced. If the chamber surface is damaged, the entire barrel must be replaced.

4. Failure to Eject. Ejection of a cartridge is an element in the cycle of functioning of the rifle, regardless of the mode of fire. A malfunction occurs when the cartridge is not ejected through the ejection port and either remains partly in the chamber or becomes jammed in the upper receiver as the bolt closes. When the firer initially clears the rifle, the cartridge could strike an inside surface of the receiver and bounce back into the path of the bolt.

Probable Cause. The cartridge must extract before it can eject. Failures to eject can also be caused by a buildup of carbon or fouling on the ejector spring or extractor, or from short recoil. Short recoil is usually due to a buildup of fouling in the carrier mechanism or gas tube, which could result in many failures to include a failure to eject. Resistance caused by a carbon-coated or corroded chamber can impede the extraction, and then the ejection of a cartridge.

Corrective Action. While retraction of the charging handle usually frees the cartridge and permits removal, the charging handle must not be released until the position of the next live round is determined. If another live round has been sufficiently stripped from the magazine or remains in the chamber, then the magazine and all live rounds could also require removal before the charging handle can be released. If several malfunctions occur and are not corrected by cleaning and lubricating, the ejector spring, extractor spring, and extractor should be replaced.

5. Other Malfunctions. The following paragraphs describe some other malfunctions that can occur.
1. The bolt fails to remain in a rearward position after the last round in the magazine is fired. Check for a bad magazine or short recoil.
2. The bolt fails to lock in the rearward position when the bolt catch has been engaged. Check bolt catch; turn in to unit armorer.
3. The trigger fails to pull or return after release with the selector set in a firing position. This indicates that the trigger pin has backed out of the receiver or the hammer spring is broken. Turn in to armorer to replace or repair.

4. The magazine fails to lock into the magazine well. Check the magazine and magazine catch for damage. Turn in to armorer to adjust the catch; replace as required.
5. Any part of the bolt carrier group fails to function. Check for incorrect assembly of components. Correctly clean and assemble the bolt carrier group or replace damaged parts.
6. The ammunition fails to feed from the magazine. Check for damaged magazine. A damaged magazine could cause repeated feeding failures and should be turned in to the armorer or exchanged.

Misfire Procedures

Stuck Cartridge: Some swelling of the cartridge occurs when it fires. If the swelling is excessive, the cartridge will be fixed tightly in the chamber. If the extractor spring has weakened and does not tightly grip the base of the cartridge, it may fail to extract a round when the bolt moves to the rear. Clear the weapon prior to this corrective action.

Ensure the bolt is held to the rear and use the cleaning rod to punch down from the muzzle to dislodge the stuck casing. Prior to doing these actions, allow the weapon to cool if at all possible.

Ruptured Cartridge: Sometimes a cartridge is in a weakened condition after firing. In addition, it may swell as described above. In this case, a properly functioning extractor may sometimes tear the base of the cartridge off as the bolt moves to the rear, leaving the rest of the cartridge wedged inside the chamber. The ruptured cartridge extractor must be used in this instance to remove it.

Clear the weapon; disassemble the weapon by removing the bolt carrier. Insert the shell extractor, which is attached to the cleaning rod, into the chamber to grip and remove the remains of the cartridge. Inspect the bore and reassemble the weapon.

Troubleshooting

Problem	Check For	What To Do
Won't Fire	Selector lever on SAFE	Put it on FIRE
	Improper assembly of firing pin	Assemble correctly
	Oil or fouling in bolt	Clean with pipe cleaner
	Defective ammunition	Replace with proper ammo
	Excess carbon buildup on firing pin or in firing pin recess	Clean
Bolt Won't Lock	Dirty bolt	Clean
	Burred or broken bolt	Replace with new bolt
Failure To Extract	Broken or weak extractor spring	Replace
	Silicon insert or reinforcement ring missing from extractor	
	Dirty, corroded ammunition	Remove and discard.
	Carbon in chamber	Clean chamber
	Broken or worn extractor	Replace
	Restricted buffer assembly	Remove and clean
	Restricted movement of bolt and carrier assembly	Remove, clean, lubricate
	Clogged gas tube	Replace
	Short recoil	See below
Failure to Feed	Dirty or corroded ammunition	Remove and discard
	Dirty or damaged magazine	Clean or replace

Problem	Check For	What To Do
	Too many rounds in magazine	Remove excess rounds
	Restricted buffer assembly	Remove and clean
	Magazine not fully seated	Re-seat magazine, adjust magazine catch
	Short recoil	See below
Double Feed	Defective magazine	Replace
Failure to Chamber	Dirty or corroded ammunition	Remove and
	Carbon in carrier key or chamber	Clean
Does not Fully Lock	Dirt, corrosion, or carbon buildup in barrel locking lugs	Clean lugs
Short Recoil	Gaps in bolt rings not staggered	Stagger ring gaps
	Carbon or dirt in carrier key or on outside of gas tube	Clean
	Q-tip/pipe cleaner stuck inside carrier key	Remove
	Weak or out of spec ammunition	Replace
Bolt Fails to Lock Open After Last Round	Defective or damaged magazine	Replace
	Dirty or corroded bolt catch	Clean or Replace
	Weak or out of spec ammunition	Replace
Selector Lever Binds	Needs oil	Lubricate
	Dirt or sand under trigger	Clean

Bolt Carrier Jammed	Round jammed between bolt	See corrective action below

1- Place the firearm on SAFE.
2- Remove magazine.
3- Collapse the buttstock.
4- Push in on bottom of bolt catch.
5- While pulling down on charging handle, hit rifle butt on ground, bolt carrier should shift to rear, repeat as needed to clear the weapon.
6- While bolt is held to rear, round should fall out through magazine well.

NOTE- If this procedure fails, use a cleaning rod to push the bolt fully to the rear through the ejection port

Ammunition Warning

VSS recommends using only domestic, commercially manufactured ammunition or high-quality surplus NATO specification ammunition. Using any reloaded ammunition or any steel cased ammunition VOIDS your Limited Lifetime Warranty. When purchasing domestically produced ammunition, questions can be answered by contacting the manufacturer directly. They will have the most accurate information about their products. If you have a problem with any ammunition be sure to have the lot number from the packaging that the ammunition in question came from; the manufacturer will need this information. When purchasing surplus ammunition, it is not likely that the manufacturer is known or can be contacted. Most surplus ammunition is not from questionable sources, but some surplus ammunition is from rejected lots that did not meet a required specification. Find out as much as you can or purchase a small sample of the surplus ammunition before purchasing larger quantities. Many message boards will also have posts with reviews on ammunition by members. While these resources do not represent the final authority in ammunition related issues, they serve as a helpful guide for general information concerning various types of ammunition. Before Firing Any Ammunition, inspect each cartridge for defects.

Dispose of cartridges that exhibit and of the following defects:
- Deformed brass. Including burrs, cracks, dents, scratches, bent or bowed cases.
- Deformed bullet. Including burrs, dents and scratches.
- Improperly seated bullets. The case neck should be uniform with no deformations and the bullet should be seated tightly in the case. Check overall length to ensure the bullet is not seated too deeply or has been pushed in from an impact. Some ammunition may have a colored sealant around the case neck.
- Improperly seated primers. The primer should be flush with the base of the case with no visible damage to the primer cup. Some ammunition may have a colored sealant around the primer.
- Corroded cartridges. Any amount of metal that is corroded and eaten away.
- Do not fire cartridges exposed to extreme heat (135 F°) until they have cooled.

Warning Signs

Not all defective ammunition has visible traits to distinguish it from good ammunition. If any cartridge from a lot of ammunition exhibits any of the following characteristics, discontinue the use of the entire lot and contact the manufacturer or dispose of the ammunition properly.

1. **Inconsistent function**. This can also be a firearm related malfunction. Clean and test the rifle with another source of ammunition. If proper function is restored discontinue the use of the suspect ammunition immediately.
2. **Blown primers**. This is an indication of improper powder charge. Discontinue the use of the suspect ammunition immediately.
3. **Inconsistent sound**. Noticeably louder or quieter reports indicate improper powder charge. Discontinue the use of the suspect ammunition immediately.
4. **Cartridge fails to chamber**. This can also be a firearm related malfunction. Clean and test the rifle with another source of ammunition. If proper function is restored discontinue the use of the suspect ammunition immediately.

Other ammunition related problems can occur. If you believe that ammunition you are using is performing in an inconsistent manner, do not take any chances that you are experiencing a one-off occurrence. Discontinue the use of the suspect ammunition and contact the manufacturer.

www.ingramcontent.com/pod-product-compliance
Lightning Source LLC
Chambersburg PA
CBHW040936110426
42739CB00026B/9